owning a pet
RABBIT

David and Penny Glover

W
FRANKLIN WATTS
LONDON • SYDNEY

First published in 2005 by
Franklin Watts
96 Leonard Street
London
EC2A 4XD

Franklin Watts Australia
45–51 Huntley Street
Alexandria, NSW 2015

© Franklin Watts 2005

Series editor: Adrian Cole
Series design: Sarah Borny
Art director: Jonathan Hair
Picture researcher: Kathy Lockley
Special photography: Adelle Homer
Illustrations by: Hannah Matthews

A CIP catalogue record for this book is
available from the British Library.

ISBN: 0 7496 5923 8

Printed in China

**This book is dedicated to the memory of Daisy,
the black and white Dutch.**

Acknowledgements:

Ron Chapple/Alamy Images 29.
Musee Condee, Chantilly/Giraudon/Bridgeman Art Library 8 br
Adelle Homer title page, 5, 10, 11 t, 11 b, 12 t, 12 b, 13 t, 14 t, 14 b,
15 t, 15 b, 16 b, 17 bl, 17 br, 17 t, 18 b, 18 t, 19, 20 t, 20 bl, 20 br, 21
t, 21 b, 23 t, 23 b, 24, 25 b, 27 t and Cover.
Klein/ Still Pictures 16 t. Michael Leach/N.H.P.A. 26 r.
William Paton/N.H.P.A. 7. Rod Planck/N.H.P.A. 4 tr.
Rex Features 9, 27 b. Matthew Richardson /Alamy Images 25 t.
John Shaw/ N.H.P.A. 4 bl. Harald Theissen/Alamy Images 28.
Maximilian Weinzierl/Alamy Images 13 b.

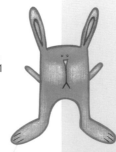

Contents

Pet rabbits

Rabbits are gentle, affectionate and lively. They are kept as pets by millions of people worldwide – but they need commitment, attention and care.

Rabbits worldwide

There are many different types of wild rabbit found in North America, Europe and Australia. Rabbits have become extinct in most of Central Asia. The Ryukyu rabbit, found in Japan, is one of the most endangered rabbits. Rabbits are not rodents, as many people believe. They belong to a different family of mammals called lagomorphs. Rodents only have one pair of incisors (gnawing teeth) in their top jaw, but lagomorphs have two pairs.

The rabbit's closest relatives are hares and pikas. Pikas look like small rabbits with short ears. They live in the mountains of North America.

The desert cottontail is just one of many different types of wild rabbit found in North America (see page 6). This one has left its burrow following a winter snowfall.

"A rabbit isn't easier to keep than a dog or cat. Keeping one is hard work — but worth it!" Jack and Daisy

What a rabbit needs

Rabbits are not as easy to keep as you might think. A rabbit does not enjoy being kept in a hutch or cage all day. It needs: lots of exercise; toys to play with; a clean, safe home; a balanced diet and careful handling. It relies on its owner for all of these.

DUTY OF CARE

RSPCA International has outlined five basic rights that should be granted to all pets:

- **Freedom from hunger and thirst**
- **Freedom from discomfort**
- **Freedom from pain, injury and disease**
- **Freedom to express normal behaviour**
- **Freedom from fear and distress**

Is a rabbit right for me?

Everyone loves rabbits, after all they are incredibly cute, but this shouldn't be your only reason for keeping one. Don't forget that rabbits live for 5–10 years, leave fur on the carpet, chew things, dig up plants and don't really like to be picked up. But if you have the time and patience to give a rabbit the care and respect it deserves, then maybe a bunny is the pet for you.

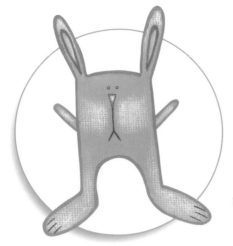

Wild rabbits!

All pet rabbits are descendents of wild European rabbits. These were originally found in the Mediterranean area of southern Spain.

The colony

In the wild, rabbits live in colonies. A typical colony contains about 30 individuals. Their home, called a warren, is a network of connecting tunnels, boltholes and dens that may have been dug by many generations of rabbits. A rabbit digs its burrow with its strong front claws. The doe (female) does most of the work.

COTTONTAILS

Some wild rabbits in North America are called 'cottontails'. They have a tail that is brown on top but white underneath. They include the marsh rabbit, swamp rabbit and the desert cottontail.

This rabbit has dug a burrow in a bank of soft earth. Rabbits like to dig in earth or sand, but avoid soil that is too wet or filled with clay.

Rabbit habits

Wild rabbits usually feed on grass and other plants from dusk to dawn, although they sometimes feed during the day if they are undisturbed. They stay within about 50 metres of their warren. Here, they can also run and play in relative safety. Rabbits constantly listen for danger (a passing fox, for example) with their sensitive ears. At the first sign of trouble a rabbit stamps its back feet in warning and flashes its tail, causing all the rabbits to bolt for the nearest hole.

A REAL PEST

For many farmers in Australia wild rabbits are a real pest, causing about A$600 million worth of damage to crops every year. In 1859, just 24 rabbits were introduced to Australia by a farmer called Thomas Austin. By 1900 there were millions of them! Rabbits also compete with the farmers' livestock by eating the grass, which holds the sandy soil together. But they are just doing what comes naturally – rabbits are one of nature's true survivors.

Rabbits are territorial. They mark the area around their home by spraying urine and by marking with scent from special glands under their chin.

Rabbit history

For hundreds of years people have valued rabbits for their fur and meat. It is only recently that people have learnt to love rabbits as pets. But even now they are still used for other purposes.

From food to friend

The Romans (510 BCE–476 CE) were the first people to breed and farm rabbits for their meat and fur. They took them from Spain to Italy and France – but not to Britain. Most people believe wild British rabbits are descended from rabbits introduced later by the Normans.

In the 15th century, domesticated rabbits were raised as pets in monasteries in France (left). However, it was not until the 16th century that pet rabbits began to be widely accepted.

Fertility symbol

Rabbits are well-known for their ability to breed quickly. In fact, a mature doe can produce several litters of 6–8 babies each year. This has led many cultures to see rabbits as a symbol of fertility and rebirth. The most familiar of these symbols appears during the spring festival of Easter – the Easter bunny. It originates from the tale of a bird that wanted to become a rabbit. When it was turned into a bunny it laid eggs every spring to say thank you.

This is a chocolate Easter bunny!

Animal testing

Rabbits have very sensitive eyes and skin. Unfortunately, this makes them attractive for use in many laboratory tests. Animal rights groups believe all animals should be free and that these tests are cruel. Other people argue the tests are necessary, usually because they feel the tests will help to save human lives in the future. Many cosmetic companies have stopped testing their products on animals.

Many animal rights campaigners protest about the tests that still go on in laboratories today.

Choosing a rabbit

Domestic rabbits come in a variety of colours and sizes. There are more than 50 recognised breeds. These have been produced over many generations by selective breeding from wild rabbits.

The first decision you need to make is whether you want a young rabbit or an adult. Adults are a better choice if you are in a family with young children. They are less destructive and easier to toilet train. If you get a young rabbit you can grow up with it every step of the way. It will be very energetic, but more vulnerable to illnesses. You also need to know how big it will grow! Domestic rabbits range in size from 'dwarf' breeds that can fit in your hand, to beefy bunnies bigger than human babies.

DUTCH

Size: .... **small**

Grooming: ...... **easy**

Varieties: .... **black, blue, chocolate, grey, steel and tortoise on white**

Description: .... **Calm, sociable, very popular first rabbit**

Dutch

Dutch rabbits, as the name suggests, originate from the Netherlands. They were first bred there in the 15th century for their beautiful banded coat. They are the world's number one choice for a pet rabbit.

ENGLISH SPOT

Size: .... **medium**

Grooming: ...... **easy**

Varieties: .... **blue, chocolate, gold, grey, lilac and tortoise on white**

Description: ..... **very sociable, relaxed, popular first rabbit**

KEEPING A PAIR

You can keep two rabbits together but they should be: two females; a spayed female and a neutered male; or two neutered males. This will prevent any unwanted breeding and reduce aggressive male behaviour.

English Spot

These rabbits have been made very popular by their unusual markings. The English Spot originates from the English Butterfly rabbit and was first seen around the 1850s.

BELGIAN HARE

Size: .... **medium**

Grooming: ...... **easy**

Varieties: .... **standard red/black**

Description: ... **curious, need lots of attention, easily scared**

Belgian Hare

These medium-sized rabbits with long legs and ears look more like hares than rabbits, hence their name, but they are true rabbits. Belgian Hares were amongst the first rabbits to be kept as pets.

Choosing a rabbit

Netherland Dwarfs are the roundest rabbits of all!

NETHERLAND DWARF

Size: .... **dwarf**

Grooming: .... **easy**

Varieties include: ... **black, blue, chinchilla, opal, pearl, seal, tan and white**

Description: .... **some have a bad temper, but most are very playful**

Netherland Dwarf

These are the smallest, roundest rabbits and are available in 32 varieties. They were first bred in the Netherlands in the early 1900s, before being further developed in the UK and USA. They are highly intelligent and quickly learn to respond to their name. They can also be easily toilet trained.

Rex

The Rex, or 'Casterex' as it was called originally, was bred in France from wild grey rabbits. It was first seen at a rabbit show in 1924. The Rex is easily recognised by its dense, velvet-like fur and short curly whiskers. The Rex is also available in a dwarf variety, which was first bred in the USA.

REX

Size: ....**large**

Grooming: .... **easy**

Varieties include: **black, blue, chocolate, black otter, castor, lilac, lynx, opal, red, sable, seal and white**

Description: ..... **generally very friendly, less active, make good first rabbits**

NETHERLAND DWARF LOP

Size: .... **dwarf**

Grooming:............ **medium**

Varieties include: ... **agouti, pointed white, self and wide band**

Description:.......... **calm, although some can be easily scared**

Take expert advice

Make contact with a rabbit club. They can help you choose a breed, put you in touch with reputable and caring breeders or a rabbit rescue centre. Most experts suggest that you should not buy your rabbit from a pet shop. This is because rabbits are very sensitive, and transporting them and changing their diet frequently may cause health problems, such as stress.

Netherland Dwarf Lop

This dwarf lop was first recognised in the Netherlands in 1964. Although not a strict 'dwarf' breed, they have great characters and are a popular first choice.

DWARF ANGORA

Size: .... **medium**

Grooming:............ **difficult**

Varieties include: .... **agouti, self, shaded and ticked**

Description: .... **very calm, less active, love to be groomed**

Dwarf Angora

The Dwarf Angora was first bred in the USA in the 1970s, where it was called the 'Jersey Woolly'. Today, it is a popular choice of rabbit because of its lush fur, calm nature and manageable size.

A good home

Rabbits can live indoors or outdoors, but they should always be in a safe environment where they have space to move around easily.

What size?

Rabbits need exercise to stay healthy, so choose a hutch or cage that is as big as possible. It must be big enough for your rabbit to stand on its hind legs and hop in any direction once it is fully grown.

POSITION

Position the hutch out of the wind and rain, and so that it is not exposed to strong sunlight all day.

HUTCH STRUCTURE

Your hutch must be made from strong wood, and be divided into two parts – an 'outdoor' area where your rabbit can feed and spend the day and a sleeping area where it can hide and feel safe. The outdoor area should have a wire front, with small holes so that vermin cannot get inside.

FLOOR

Buy a hutch with a wooden floor at least 1cm thick. A wire floor will make your rabbit's feet sore.

DOOR

The door should have strong, secure latches.

LEGS

Stand your hutch on legs, or on a table, to keep it out of the reach of animals such as cats and foxes.

"Rabbits are curious and like to gnaw and dig. You must bunny-proof all the rooms your rabbit has access to."

House rabbits

Rabbits are very clean, so keeping a house rabbit has become very popular. You can train your rabbit to use a litter tray in the corner of a room, like a cat – but use newspaper covered with hay or straw, not cat litter. Make sure electric wires are protected by plastic piping and that your rabbit has a digging box filled with sand or soil. Close the bathroom door to stop your rabbit jumping in the toilet and block off small areas, such as behind the sofa, so your rabbit can't get trapped.

HOUSE RABBIT CAGES

A cage should:

- **have plenty of headroom for your rabbit**
- **be positioned in a safe place out of draughts and direct sunlight**
- **be made from a strong metal mesh, with a deep plastic tray**
- **have a large, side-opening door and one at the top, too**

RABBIT RUN

A run is a safe place for your rabbit to hop about in if you don't have an escape-proof garden. A permanent rabbit run must always be covered with wood and wire mesh panels on the top as well as the sides. The wire mesh must be dug into the ground by at least 30cm to stop your rabbit digging out, or predators digging in. Portable dog fences are a good temporary solution.

Food and water

Rabbits are herbivores, which means they only eat plants. Wild rabbits graze on the grass and other plants around their warrens at dawn and dusk.

The main part of a pet rabbit's diet is fresh grass hay, not straw or alfalfa. It should always be available in its hutch or cage. Hay must be supplemented with high-quality rabbit pellets (15–18% protein and about 18% fibre). Feed these to your rabbit in the morning and again in the evening.

Your rabbit will also enjoy some fresh vegetables, such as sliced carrot, and a small amount of fruit, such as apple slices. Other treats include dried banana pieces and raisins. Food that is too watery, such as lettuce leaves, could give your rabbit diarrhoea. Never feed your rabbit sweets or leftovers from meals.

Rabbit digestion

Rabbits have a big stomach so they can eat large amounts of food quickly. But their stomach is delicate and can be easily upset. Check your rabbit's droppings, they are a good indication of how your bunny is feeling.

BIG BUNNIES

Don't overfeed your rabbit either. Regularly check its size: if it feels too thin or fat around its ribs, increase or decrease the amount of food it is given. If you are unsure, check with your vet.

Rabbits should eat a well-balanced diet made up of grass hay, high-quality pellets, fresh vegetables and water.

"A rabbit's food bowl should be heavy and hard to tip over."

To stay healthy, rabbits need a well-balanced, nutritious diet. Always check your rabbit to make sure it is feeding properly.

Water

Your rabbit must always have fresh water to drink. A drip-feed bottle is better than a bowl, which can easily be contaminated. Watch to make sure it is positioned where your rabbit can drink from it easily. Clean and refill your rabbit's water every day, and twice a day during hot weather. When you put your rabbit in its run, make sure that it has water there, too.

Rabbit poo

Rabbits produce two kinds of poo, or droppings, from their food: hard round droppings that you normally see (below); and softer, smellier droppings called caecotrophs (also spelt cecotropes). The rabbit eats these soft droppings, usually at night, so its digestive system can absorb the goodness they contain. It's quite normal for your rabbit to do this, but you should consult your vet if it happens continually. It could be a sign that your rabbit is receiving an unbalanced diet.

Rabbits must always have access to clean water – even when you place them in their run.

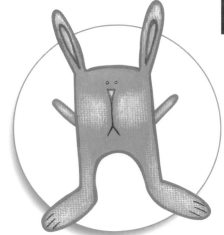

New skills

Getting to know your new rabbit is an exciting time – they have very complicated personalities! It is important to give your rabbit the right sort of attention as it grows up.

Bonding with your bunny

Try to feed your rabbit at the same times every day. It will come to know the routine. Talk to it and move slowly and gently as you change the food and water. Avoid sudden movements and loud noises that could easily scare it. Offer your rabbit food to eat, holding it still until it is confident enough to take them.

Handling your rabbit

Most rabbits do not like to be picked up, cuddled or carried and will probably struggle and kick.

It's better to let your rabbit come to you. Try experimenting by lying on the floor – it won't be too long before your rabbit comes to investigate. Never pick up a rabbit by its ears, or just by the scruff of the neck. You will hurt it and may cause permanent damage. Always support its weight from underneath – holding gently onto the loose skin behind the head, if necessary.

BEHAVIOUR GUIDE

It can be tricky to know what your rabbit is trying to say. Here are some general ideas:

Grunting Soft grunts usually indicate happiness. Loud grunts are a warning – something is upsetting the rabbit and it is about to attack.

Standing Rabbits stand up on their hind legs to get a better view of things – just as they would in the wild.

Running and skipping Rabbits like to run and skip around things, including you. They do this when they're enjoying themselves.

Teeth grinding or purring A rabbit gently grinds its teeth to make a purring noise when it is happy. A loud grinding sound can indicate that it's not feeling well.

Squealing A rabbit squeals when it's in pain or really scared. Your rabbit may do this when you pick it up.

Chinning Rabbits rub the scent glands on their chin on items to indicate that they belong to them – they will even mark you!

Thumping Rabbits thump their feet when they feel frightened or they think they're in danger.

STROKING

Some rabbits don't enjoy being stroked – and they all hate being touched on their nose, mouth and rear. Try gently stroking your rabbit on its head, moving your hand in the same direction as the fur. If it closes its eyes or lies down, you know it's happy with you doing it. Talk softly to your rabbit as you stroke it.

PLAYTIME

Rabbits are very playful and they also enjoy chewing on things. Toys, such as rubber balls and even cardboard tubes, provide a great distraction from the sofa and chair legs.

Toys provide mental stimulation – a bored rabbit is an unhappy rabbit. Give your rabbit toys to play with, but don't overcrowd it.

Staying healthy

Rabbits are by nature very clean animals – they like to keep themselves and their home tidy. A clean home will help to keep your rabbit happy, healthy and in good condition.

GOOD HYGIENE

Keep your rabbit's bedding fresh and dry and clear up spilled food and water daily. Rabbits usually choose one area of the hutch or cage to use as a toilet, and you should clean this up daily. Rabbits do not usually soil the bedding in the sleeping area. Regular cleaning helps to reduce the risk of disease.

Don't forget to wash your hands after cleaning your rabbit's hutch or cage to reduce the risk of spreading germs.

RABBIT MANICURE

A rabbit's claws never stop growing. If you allow your rabbit plenty of time to scratch around in the garden, its claws will usually wear down by themselves. However, most house rabbits' claws will need clipping – you should check them every 6–8 weeks. You can clip the claws yourself, but if you don't feel confident enough, ask an experienced rabbit-keeper or a vet to do the job.

CLEANING

If your hutch is outside, clean it out at least once a week, or as soon as you see it getting dirty. If your garden is rabbit-proof, let your bunny out for some exercise while you give the hutch a good scrub with non-toxic detergent and hot water. Make sure the hutch is thoroughly dry before you let your rabbit back in.

If you have a house rabbit you should clean its cage every day.

EXERCISE

Give your rabbit the chance to run around and explore as often as possible, whether in an escape-proof garden, in a run or indoors. Without proper exercise – 3 to 4 hours a day – a rabbit becomes bored and depressed. Don't forget to give it a few toys to play with.

WASHING

Never give a rabbit a bath – it can cause distress and send it into shock. If your rabbit gets dirty, give it a gentle rub down with a clean, damp cloth.

GROOMING

Rabbits groom their own fur to keep it clean and in good condition. However, unlike cats, rabbits cannot cough up furballs that form in their throat (see page 25). You can help by brushing your rabbit gently with a rabbit brush every week. Long-haired rabbits need to be brushed at least once a day.

Visiting the vet

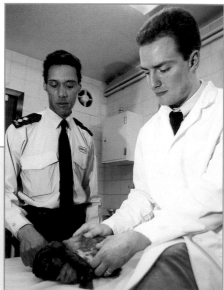

It can be quite difficult to tell if your rabbit is sick. It is up to you to monitor its behaviour, so that if it does fall ill, you can act as quickly as possible. Even a well cared for rabbit can become ill.

SIGNS YOUR BUNNY MAY BE POORLY:

- **Severe diarrhoea (soft smelly droppings or droppings covered with mucus)**

- **Loss of energy – seems unusually quiet**

- **Loss of appetite**

- **Difficulty breathing**

- **Repeated scratching (especially the ears)**

- **Inflamed eyes**

- **Discharge from the nostrils and sneezing**

At the vet

The vet will examine your rabbit, and ask you about its symptoms. How has your rabbit's behaviour changed? Has it eaten anything unusual? When the vet has diagnosed the problem, he or she will tell you how your rabbit should be treated. Listen carefully to any instructions your vet gives you, and write them down if necessary.

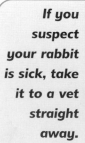

If you suspect your rabbit is sick, take it to a vet straight away.

Fleas

Your rabbit may pick up fleas from other animals. If it seems uncomfortable or is repeatedly scratching itself, check around its ears and neck. Treat your rabbit with flea powder, as directed by your vet, as soon as possible. Clean its hutch or cage thoroughly. If you have a house rabbit you may need to move its cage to another room and treat the carpet, too.

If you discover your rabbit has fleas, treat it as soon as possible.

FLEA TREATMENT

Never use a flea collar on your rabbit. Use a rabbit flea powder as directed by your vet. You can also use a flea comb.

Vaccinations

There are vaccines for some serious rabbit illnesses, such as Myxomatosis and VHD (Viral Haemorrhagic Disease). Talk to your vet about the vaccinations recommended for your rabbit – even if you have a house rabbit.

It is your responsibility to ensure your rabbit is kept fully vaccinated. Ask your vet when boosters will be needed, and mark the dates on a calendar.

Through the year

At certain times of the year, your rabbit will need special care and attention. It is your responsibility to make sure your rabbit's condition and environment are well maintained.

Summer shade

Make sure your rabbit always has shade from the direct sun. This is especially important during the hot summer months. Check the position of the sun – your hutch may be in the shade in the morning, but what about in the afternoon? Provide your rabbit with plenty of water and a box or a cover where it can shelter.

Holiday time

Summer is the time when most people take a holiday. If you are going away, arrange for someone to look after your rabbit – perhaps a close friend or neighbour. Leave the carer a list of instructions – and don't forget to leave the vet's telephone number and address in case of an emergency.

Rabbits love to hop around in a run. Make sure they are in the shade or have somewhere to shelter from the sun.

Moulting

Towards the end of summer, your rabbit will moult, losing its fine summer coat and growing a thicker winter coat. So don't be surprised if its fur starts to come away in big clumps. House rabbits usually moult several times a year. During this time it is essential to brush your bunny frequently. This will remove the loose fur and also help to prevent problems with furballs.

FURBALLS

Furballs usually only occur as a result of poor care. If allowed to develop they will simply clog up your rabbit's gut, causing it to starve to death. Furballs can be easily avoided by regular brushing and ensuring your rabbit has access to grass hay and fresh water.

Many rabbits love to watch the TV; nobody is too sure why, though!

Preparing for winter

Generally, rabbits kept outside cope well with cold conditions because of their thick fur. However, the hutch should be completely waterproof and positioned out of cold draughts. Stock the hutch with plenty of hay and a daily supply of food and water. Rabbits don't hibernate so, if you have an escape-proof garden or run, let it out for some exercise.

During the winter

Check the hutch and remove any fallen snow from the roof. Alternatively, you could move your rabbit indoors temporarily. Make sure the house is not too hot though; a sudden rise in temperature will harm your rabbit.

Breeding rabbits?

You may consider breeding and showing rabbits. Many rabbit welfare organisations are against breeding rabbits at home. More pet rabbits are born every year than there are good homes for.

Long commitment

Breeding is not just a case of putting a doe and buck (male) together. You need the right rabbits and breeding environment. You need to be sure you can find homes for the babies. Also, consider the commitment that is required to obtain the relevant licences and bring up the young, and the extra money required for food, bedding and vet bills.

BREEDING ENVIRONMENT

Consider what you'll need before breeding rabbits:

- **A hutch for the buck measuring about 1.8 x 1 metres**

- **A hutch for the doe measuring about 1.8 x 1 metres**

- **At least 2 hutches for the babies measuring about 1.2 x 1 metres**

- **A garden to put them all in**

Breeding rabbits

The doe and buck should be high-quality or pedigree rabbits in perfect health. The doe must be at least six months old. The pregnancy usually lasts about 31 days. Rabbits normally have a litter of 6–8 babies, though 12 or more may be born. You should be prepared for the fact that if there are birthing difficulties you could lose the mother and babies.

Show rabbits

If you want to show your rabbits, it is a good idea to join a local rabbit club. There are strict rules for showing exhibition rabbits, so you should take advice from experts.

Shows are a great place to see other rabbits and to share tips – you never know, with the right preparation yours could be best in show!

Showjumping

Rabbits love to jump about and since 1979 some rabbit owners in Sweden have taught their rabbits to jump over rabbit-sized fences. Since then, rabbit showjumping has grown worldwide. The rabbits hop around a set course in timed 'events' – some just enjoy eating the grass, but it's still a great way for them to exercise.

QUICK STEPS TO GET YOUR BUNNY JUMPING

Buy a rabbit harness. The harness looks odd to start with, but most rabbits gradually get used to wearing it for short periods of time. Never use it to 'lift' your rabbit over jumps.

Make some fences. Use strong cardboard or a stick balanced between two flowerpots. Don't get disheartened if your rabbit prefers to chew the fence instead.

Practise jumping. Some rabbits will jump straight over the fences, others will need to be encouraged. Try placing some food on the other side of the fence.

Dealing with loss

Death is a fact of life, but that doesn't make it any easier to manage when your rabbit dies. Whether you expect it or not, death can still come as a shock.

The end of a life

Pet rabbits live for an average of 5–10 years. You will only really know how the death of your rabbit affects you when it happens. If you have provided the best possible care then you should not feel guilty or blame yourself – all lives eventually come to an end.

Many places have special cemeteries where people can bury their pets. Some people think it's a good way to remember their pet.

WHEN YOUR RABBIT DIES

Nothing will truly prepare you for the death of your rabbit. But these are some things to think about:

- **It sounds awful, but think about what to do with the body. If your rabbit dies at the vet's surgery he or she will usually remove the body for you. Sometimes this is the best way to say goodbye.**

- **Set up a memorial in your garden, or set aside an area in your bedroom for photographs.**

- **Talk to people about how you are feeling and share your experience with your friends.**

"I treasure every moment I have with Dusty. I know that one day she won't be there."

Sharing memories

By far the best way to cope with the death of your rabbit is to talk to people. Even if you don't think it will help, you may find that a friend has shared a similar experience.

Looking at photographs of your rabbit can help you to overcome the feeling of loss. It can also help you to remember better times.

TIME TO REMEMBER

Write a poem about your rabbit:

How do I feel? I do not know.
My heart seems to beat so slow.
I still can't believe she's not here.

How do I feel? Empty and sad.
I've never felt quite so bad.
I still want to hold her near.

How do I feel? Lonely and sour.
On her grave I lay this flower.
I still hold her memory dear.
How do I feel?

– Alison Grey, age 12

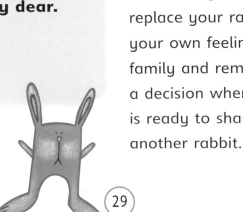

What next?

Whatever you do, don't rush out and replace your rabbit. You must consider your own feelings, and those of your family and remaining pets. Only make a decision when you are sure everyone is ready to share the joy of owning another rabbit.

Glossary

Balanced diet: A diet containing the correct mixture of different foodstuffs needed to keep an animal healthy.

Contaminated: Made dirty.

Diagnose: To find out what is wrong.

Diarrhoea: Frequently passing loose, runny droppings.

Disease: A serious illness, bad health.

Distress: Pain, disturbance, discomfort caused by bad care.

Domestic: Describes animals that are kept by people, not wild.

Dwarf: A small variety.

Endangered: Used to refer to an animal species whose numbers are becoming so low it is threatened with extinction.

Environment: The surroundings in which a rabbit (or any other creature) lives.

Generations: The successive stages of a family of living things. Parents are one generation, their offspring are the next.

Herbivore: An animal that only eats plants.

Illegal: Against the law.

Lagomorphs: The animal group to which rabbits, hares and pikas belong.

Moult: To shed and re-grow feathers, fur or skin.

Non-toxic: Not poisonous.

Nutritious: Describes good food that provides an animal with the energy and materials its body needs.

Pest: A 'destructive' animal that breeds rapidly.

RSPCA: Royal Society for the Prevention of Cruelty to Animals.

Sensitive: Easily hurt or frightened.

Symptom: A sign that an animal is ill.

Territorial: Describes an animal that guards or marks the area of land where it lives and feeds.

Vaccination: An injection to protect against some diseases.

Websites

Throughout the world there are many rabbit organisations whose members breed, show and share information about their chosen rabbit breed. Your local pet centre can provide information about local groups. Information is also available on the Internet. Some useful websites are listed below:

www.thebrc.org
This is the website of The British Rabbit Council, the leading rabbit organisation in the UK. The site includes advice for newcomers, photographs from shows, a junior site, and club and breeders directories.

www.rabbitwelfare.co.uk
The Rabbit Welfare Association aims to improve the quality of life of pet rabbits in the UK. The site features a gallery and many useful links.

www.rabbitrehome.org.uk
Rabbit Rehome UK allows rescue centres and individuals to enter details of rabbits in need of new homes. You can search for a rabbit to adopt and contact the rescue centre for further information.

www.dutchrabbits.co.uk
The United Kingdom Dutch Rabbit Club specialising in Dutch rabbits. Links to clubs for other breeds may be found at:
www.thebrc.org/links.htm

www.rabbit.org
The House Rabbit Society is an international society that rescues rabbits and provides information on rabbit care and behaviour.

More general information on the care, health and welfare of pets is available from a number of organisations. These include:

www.rspca.co.uk
The RSPCA website has links to RSPCA websites throughout the world. It is full of information about animal adoption, news, care, training and education.

www.aaps.org.au
The Australian Animal Protection Society is an independent charity that operates pet shelters. Its website has some heart-warming updates from people who have recently adopted all kinds of pets.

www.pdsa.org.uk
The Peoples' Dispensary for Sick Animals (PDSA). This organisation is a charity that provides veterinary care for sick and injured animals and promotes responsible pet ownership. Check out the 'you and your pet' section of their website.

Every effort has been made by the Publishers to ensure that these websites contain no inappropriate or offensive material. However, because of the nature of the Internet, it is impossible to guarantee that the contents of these sites will not be altered. We strongly advise that Internet access is supervised by a responsible adult.

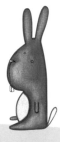

Index